COSORI AIR FRYER COOKBOOK

Deliciously Simple Recipes for Your Cosori Air Fryer

Olivia Steven

Warning-Disclaimer

The purpose of this book is to educate and entertain. The author or publisher does not guarantee that anyone following the techniques, suggestions, tips, ideas, or strategies will become successful. The author and publisher shall have neither liability or responsibility to anyone with respect to any loss or damage caused, or alleged to be caused, directly or indirectly by the information contained in this book.

CONTENTS

Poultry Recipes 23

Beef, Pork & Lamb Recipes 38

Vegetarian Recipes 48

Fish & Seafood Recipes 60

Breakfast Recipes 68

Dessert Recipes..78

INTRODUCTION

Who says that you have to give up on fried food to be healthy? Well, maybe everyone, but what those people don't know is that technology has progressed to the point where eating fried food and living healthy go hand in hand.

No, you are not dreaming, this is your dream coming true. This fantastic cookbook has different finger-licking fried meals that will not raise your cholesterol levels. These mouthwatering air fryer recipes will help you get your money's worth on your air fryer, and convince you that cooking healthy doesn't have to be expensive or time-consuming.

Satisfying all tastes, this cookbook will enrich your recipe folder with the yummiest breakfast, lunch, main dishes, side dishes, snacks, and dessert recipes, whether you are a vegetarian or a steak lover.

Show me one person who doesn't love crispy, deep-fried food. Even those who try to avoid fried food can sometimes find the urge to indulge irresistibly. And while we all lick our plates after chowing down some delicious crunchy chicken, we are all aware that besides satisfying our taste buds, fried food brings absolutely no other benefits. It increases our bad cholesterol levels, raises our blood pressure, adds more pounds to our bodies, and makes us an unhealthy, overweight nation.

But there is more than one way to fry food. Say goodbye to eating oil-soaked and calorie-loaded unhealthy food because frying with air fryer brings both, delightful flavor and health benefits.

Now, let's healthify your lifestyle, and enjoy our fried food without gaining weight.

WHY COSORI AIR FRYER?

This revolutionized kitchen appliance fries food by blowing hot air, not by dunking it in grease. The only thing you need to do is to coat the food with oil lightly, and let the air fryer do the rest. Now, you must be thinking, "but you said no oil," right? Well, here is how it works. For you to cook it, you need to coat your food with oil, but unlike the traditional way of frying in which the food soaks up all of the oil, the air fryer drains the grease while cooking. It has a built-in fan that circulates hot air around the food, and cooks it to perfection, soft on the inside, crispy and crunchy on the outside.

If this is not convincing enough for you to throw your old frying pans in the trash and introduce a new air fryer to your kitchen, then perhaps these next three most significant benefits of cooking with an air fryer will change your mind.

Cooking with Cosori Air Fryer is Healthier

Food prepared in an air fryer is 80% less greasy and just as delicious, if not even better tasting than deep-fried food. So, if you want to reduce the massive amount of fat that your favorite fried dish contains, choosing to prepare it in an air fryer is your healthier option. Cooking with an air fryer will help you lose weight without sacrificing the satisfaction and comfort of fried food.

Cooking with Cosori Air Fryer is Faster

Do you know what the best part about an air fryer is? You don't have to spend your time waiting for it to heat to the right temperature to start cooking. The air fryer can come from room temperature to more than 300 degrees F in less than a few minutes. This is a real time-saver when it comes to cooking. We all know how long it takes for a significant amount of oil to heat to the appropriate temperature for us to start deep-frying. Air fryers are also much faster than your traditional oven.

Cooking with Cosori Air Fryer is Cleaner

Aren't you tired of scrubbing all that sticky grease from the bottom of your frying pan? Or cleaning grease splatters off your stove? If so, then cooking with an air fryer will be a real enjoyment for you. Since there is literary no grease, the air fryer cleaning process is super convenient. All parts of the air fryer are easily removable and most importantly, dishwasher safe. The best way to clean it is to it with hot water and a few drops of a liquid dishwasher. Let it soak for a couple of minutes, and then wipe it with a non-abrasive sponge. Rinse under water, and voila.

And even though fried food prepared in an air fryer tastes terrific, the best part is that you can use your air fryer for so much more than making French fries. You can even prepare baked goods or roast your chicken in it.

An air fryer is super versatile, and once you get the handle of cooking with this amazing kitchen appliance, you will see that oil-free cooking can be limitless.

Here are some general air fryer cooking tips:

– Don't overcrowd the basket of the air fryer to ensure even cooking.

– You can insert any baking dish or bowl, as long as they fit in the air fryer.

– You can use aluminum foil and parchment paper just like when cooking in the oven.

– You can open the air fryer to check the doneness of the food, as many times as you like, just like you do with your oven.

– Flip the food halfway through to ensure even crispiness.

– Shake the basket of your air fryer instead of stirring frequently.

– Adding water to the drawer of the air fryer can prevent the food from getting too smoky.

– You can use your air fryer to reheat food, as well.

Crispy Potato Fries

(Prep + Cook Time: 30 minutes / Servings: 4)

Nutritional info per serving:

Calories 353, Carbohydrates 63.1g, Fat 5.5g, Protein 8.3g

Ingredients:

4 potatoes, cut into sticks
2 tbsp butter, melted
2 garlic cloves, crushed

1 tsp fresh rosemary, chopped
Salt and pepper, to taste

Directions:

1. Add butter, garlic, salt, and pepper to a bowl; toss until the sticks are well-coated.
2. Lay the potato sticks into the air fryer's basket. Cook for 15 minutes at 370 F.
3. Shake the potatoes every 5 minutes.
4. Once ready, check to ensure the fries are golden and crispy all over if not, return them to cook for a few minutes.
5. Divide standing up between metal cups lined with nonstick baking paper.
6. Serve sprinkled with rosemary.

Herby Scotch Eggs

(Prep + Cook Time: 20 minutes / Servings: 4)

Nutritional info per serving:

Calories 457, Carbohydrates 12g, Fat 37g, Protein 23g

Ingredients:

10 oz ground turkey
4 eggs, soft boiled, peeled
1 white onion, chopped
½ cup flour
2 garlic cloves, minced

2 eggs, lightly beaten
Salt and pepper to taste
½ cup breadcrumbs
1 tsp dried mixed herbs
Cooking spray

Directions:

1. Mix together the onion, garlic, salt, and pepper.

2. Shape into 4 balls.

3. Wrap the turkey mixture around each egg, and ensure the eggs are well covered.

4. Dust each egg ball in flour, then dip in the beaten eggs and finally roll in the crumbs, until coated.

5. Spray with cooking spray.

6. Lay the eggs into your Air fryer's basket.

7. Set the temperature to 390 degrees F and cook for 15 minutes.

8. After 8 minutes, turn the eggs.

9. Slice in half and serve warm.

Honey-Thyme Eggplant Chips

(Prep + Cook Time: 20 minutes / Servings: 4)

Nutritional info per serving:

Calories 287, Carbohydrates 31.1g, Fat 15.8g, Protein 3.3g

Ingredients:

2 eggplants
2 tsp honey
⅓ cup olive oil
⅓ cup cornstarch

½ cup water
1 tsp dry thyme
A pinch of salt

Directions:

1. Preheat the Cosori Air Fryer to 370°F. Cut the eggplants in slices of ½ -inch each.

2. In a big bowl, mix the cornstarch, water, olive oil, and eggplant slices, until evenly coated.

3. Line the air fryer basket with baking paper and spray with olive oil. Place the eggplants in the basket, scatter with thyme and cook for 15 minutes on Air Fry mode, shaking every 5 minutes.

4. When ready, transfer the eggplants to a serving platter and drizzle with honey.

5. Serve with yogurt dip.

Asparagus & Bacon Wraps

(Prep + Cook Time: 30 minutes / Servings: 6)

Nutritional info per serving:

Calories 271, Carbohydrates 10.2g, Fat 25.3g, Protein 12.5g

Ingredients:

1 lb asparagus spears, trimmed
1 lb bacon, sliced
½ cup Parmesan cheese, grated

Cooking spray
Salt and pepper, to taste

Directions:

1. Preheat the Cosori Air Fryer to 370 F.
2. Place the bacon slices out on a work surface, top each one with one asparagus spear and half of the cheese. Wrap the bacon around the asparagus.
3. Line the air fryer basket with parchment paper.
4. Arrange the wraps into the basket, scatter over the remaining cheese, season with salt and black pepper, and spray with cooking spray.
5. Cook for 8 to 10 minutes on Roast mode. If necessary work in batches. Serve hot!

Cheesy Cauliflower Bites

(Prep + Cook Time: 45 minutes / Servings: 8)

Nutritional info per serving:

Calories 121, Carbohydrates 8.4g, Fat 7.2g, Protein 7.2g

Ingredients:

2 cups cauliflower florets, steamed
1 egg
3 ½ oz oats
1 red onion, diced

1 tsp mustard
5 oz cheddar cheese
Salt and pepper, to taste

Directions:

1. Preheat the Cosori Air Fryer to 350 degrees F.
2. Add the oats in a food processor and process until they resemble breadcrumbs.
3. Place the steamed florets in a cheesecloth and squeeze out the excess liquid.
4. Put the florets in a large bowl, and add the rest of the ingredients to the bowl.
5. Mix well with your hands, to combine the ingredients thoroughly.
6. Take a little bit of the mixture and twist it into a straw.
7. Place in the lined air fryer basket; repeat with the rest of the mixture.
8. Cook for 10 minutes on Air Fry mode.
9. After 5 minutes, turn them over and cook for an additional 10 minutes.

Broccoli and Gruyère Tater Tots

(Prep + Cook Time: 35 minutes / Servings: 10)

Nutritional info per serving:

Calories 132, Carbohydrates 10.9g, Fat 5.2g, Protein 6.4g

Ingredients:

2 lb broccoli florets, steamed
5 oz Gruyère cheese
1 onion, diced
1 cup breadcrumbs
1 egg, beaten

1 tsp chopped parsley
1 tsp chopped oregano
1 tsp chopped chives
1 tsp garlic powder
Salt and pepper, to taste

Directions:

1. Mash the broccoli and place it in a large bowl.
2. Add the onion, parsley, oregano, chives, garlic powder, salt, and pepper, and gruyère cheese. Mix with hands until thoroughly combined.
3. Form 12 balls out of the mixture. Line a baking sheet with paper.
4. Dip half of the tater tots into the egg and then coat with breadcrumbs.
5. Arrange them on the baking sheet and cook in the air fryer at 350 F for 15 minutes on Air Fry mode. Repeat with the other half.

Buttered Mushrooms

(Prep + Cook Time: 20 minutes / Servings: 4)

Nutritional info per serving:

Calories 123, Carbohydrates 3.5g, Fat 11.8g, Protein 2.8g

Ingredients:

2 rosemary sprigs
12 oz button mushrooms
¼ cup melted butter

½ tsp salt
¼ tsp black pepper
3 garlic cloves, minced

Directions:

1. Preheat the Cosori Air Fryer to 350 degrees F.
2. Wash and pat dry the mushrooms and cut them in half. Place in a large bowl.
3. Add the remaining ingredients to the bowl and toss well to combine.
4. Transfer the mushrooms to the basket of the air fryer.
5. Cook for 12 minutes on Air Fry mode, shaking once halfway through.

Cheesy New York Steak

(Prep + Cook Time: 15 minutes / Servings: 4)

Nutritional info per serving:

Calories 316, Carbohydrates 13.3g, Fat 16.5g, Protein 22.8g

Ingredients:

2 New York strip steaks
12 kalamata olives
8 oz halloumi cheese
2 tbsp chopped parsley

2 tbsp chopped mint
Juice and zest of 1 lemon
Salt and pepper, to taste
Olive oil

Directions:

1. Preheat the Cosori Air Fryer to 350 degrees F.
2. Season the steaks with salt and pepper, and gently brush with olive oil.
3. Place into the Air fryer and cook for 6 minutes (for medium rare) on Air Fry mode. When ready, remove to a plate and set aside.
4. Drizzle the cheese with olive oil and place it in the Air fryer; cook for 4 minutes.
5. Remove to a serving platter and serve with sliced steaks and olives, sprinkled with herbs, and lemon zest and juice.

Parmesan Meatballs

(Prep + Cook Time: 30 minutes / Servings: 6)

Nutritional info per serving:

Calories 528, Carbohydrates 76.4g, Fat 17.8g, Protein 21g

Ingredients:

2 lb ground beef	½ tsp salt
1 potato, shredded	Cooking spray
2 eggs, beaten	½ cup Parmesan cheese, grated
2 tbsp chopped chives	1 package cooked spaghetti to serve
¼ tsp pepper	2 cups tomato sauce to serve
½ tsp garlic powder	Basil leaves to serve

Directions:

1. Preheat the Cosori Air Fryer to 330 degrees F.
2. In a large bowl, combine the potato, salt, pepper, garlic powder, eggs, and chives.
3. Form 12 balls out of the mixture. Spray with cooking spray.
4. Arrange half of the balls onto a lined air fryer basket.
5. Cook for 14 minutes on Air Fry mode. After 7 minutes, turn the meatballs.
6. Repeat with the other half. Serve over cooked spaghetti mixed with tomato sauce, sprinkled with Parmesan cheese and basil leaves.

Dijon Cheesy Cookies

(Prep + Cook Time: 50 minutes / Servings: 6)

Nutritional info per serving:

Calories 411, Carbohydrates 19.9g, Fat 28.4g, Protein 17.7g

Ingredients:

1 sheet puff pastry	1 ½ cups Gruyere cheese, grated
8 ham slices	4 tsp Dijon mustard

Directions:

1. Preheat the Cosori Air Fryer to 370 degrees F.
2. Place the pastry on a lightly floured flat surface.
3. Brush the mustard over and arrange the ham slices; top with cheese.
4. Start at the shorter edge and roll up the pastry.
5. Wrap it in a plastic foil and place in the freezer for about half an hour, until it becomes firm and comfortable to cut.
6. Meanwhile, slice the pastry into 6 rounds.
7. Line the air fryer basket with parchment paper, and arrange the pinwheels on top.
8. Cook for 10 minutes on Air Fry mode. Leave to cool on a wire rack before serving.

Brussels Sprouts with Cherries

(Prep + Cook Time: 45 minutes / Servings: 4)

Nutritional info per serving:

Calories 211, Carbohydrates 22.1g, Fat 13.5g, Protein 5.1g

Ingredients:

14 oz Brussels sprouts, steamed
2 oz Cherries, dried
1 tbsp olive oil

Juice and zest of 1 orange
2 oz toasted pine nuts

Directions:

1. Soak the dried cherries in the orange juice and let sit for about 20 minutes.
2. Preheat the Cosori Air Fryer to 370 degrees F.
3. Drizzle the Brussels sprouts with the olive oil, and place them in the basket of the air fryer.
4. Cook for 15 minutes on Air Fry mode.
5. Remove to a bowl and top with pine nuts, cherries, and orange zest.

Garlicky Baked Baby Carrots

(Prep + Cook Time: 25 minutes / Servings: 4)

Nutritional info per serving:

Calories 124, Carbohydrates 13.7g, Fat 6.9g, Protein 1.8g

Ingredients:

1 ¼ lb baby carrots
2 tbsp olive oil
1 tsp cumin seeds
½ tsp cumin powder

½ tsp garlic powder
1 handful cilantro, chopped
1 tsp salt
½ tsp black pepper

Directions:

1. Preheat the Cosori Air Fryer to 370 degrees F.
2. Place the baby carrots in a large bowl.
3. Add cumin seeds, cumin, olive oil, salt, garlic powder, and pepper, and stir to coat them well.
4. Put the carrots in the air fryer's basket, and cook for 20 minutes on Roast mode.
5. Remove to a platter and sprinkle with chopped cilantro, to serve.

Dilled Cod Skewers

(Prep + Cook Time: 75 minutes / Servings: 4)

Nutritional info per serving:

Calories 176, Carbohydrates 2g, Fat 17g, Protein 16g

Ingredients

3 tbsp olive oil
2 garlic cloves, grated
1 tsp dill, chopped
Salt to taste

1 lemon, juiced and zested
1 lemon, cut in wedges to serve
1 pound cod loin, boneless, skinless, cubed

Directions:

1. In a bowl, combine the olive oil, garlic, dill, salt, and lemon juice.
2. Stir in the cod and place in the fridge to marinate for 1 hour.
3. Preheat your Cosori Air Fryer to 390°F. Thread the cod pieces onto halved skewers.
4. Arrange into the oiled air fryer basket; cook for 10 minutes. Flip them over halfway through cooking.
5. When ready, remove to a serving platter, scatter lemon zest and serve with wedges.

Paprika Cabbage with Parmesan

(Prep + Cook Time: 30 minutes / Servings: 4)

Nutritional info per serving:

Calories 245, Carbohydrates 7.4g, Fat 19.4g, Protein 12.2g

Ingredients:

½ head cabbage, cut into 4 wedges
4 tbsp butter, melted
2 cup Parmesan cheese

Salt and pepper, to taste
1 tsp smoked paprika

Directions:

1. Preheat the Cosori Air Fryer to 330 F. Line the basket with parchment paper.
2. Brush the butter over the cabbage wedges; season with salt and pepper.
3. Coat the cabbage with the Parmesan cheese.
4. Arrange in the basket and sprinkle with paprika.
5. Cook for 15 minutes on Air Fry mode, flip over and cook for an additional 10 minutes.

Tomato & Mozzarella Ciabatta Sandwich

(Prep + Cook Time: 15 minutes / Servings: 2)

Nutritional info per serving:

Calories 215, Carbohydrates 17g, Fat 5.6g, Protein 23.5g

Ingredients:

1 Italian Ciabatta Sandwich Bread
Olive oil to brush
2 tomatoes, chopped
2 garlic cloves, minced

1 cup grated mozzarella cheese
Basil leaves, chopped
Salt and pepper to taste

Directions:

1. Preheat your Cosori Air Fryer to 380 degrees F.
2. Cut the bread in half, lengthways, then each piece again in half. Drizzle each bit with olive oil and sprinkle with garlic. Top with the grated cheese, salt, and pepper.
3. Place the bruschetta pieces into the air fryer basket and cook for 12 minutes on Air Fry mode. After 6 minutes, check for doneness.
4. Once the air fryer beeps, remove the bruschetta to a serving platter, spoon over the tomatoes and chopped basil to serve.

POULTRY RECIPES

Lemony Chicken Schnitzels

(Prep + Cook Time: 25 minutes / Servings: 4)

Nutritional info per serving:

Calories 513, Carbohydrates 44g, Fat 28g, Protein 49g

Ingredients:

4 chicken breasts, boneless
1 cup flour
2 eggs, beaten
1 cup breadcrumbs
Salt and pepper to taste

2 tbsp fresh parsley, chopped
4 slices cold butter
4 slices lemon
Cooking spray

Directions:

1. Preheat your Cosori Air Fryer to 380 degrees F.
2. Combine the breadcrumbs with the parsley in a dish and set aside.
3. Season the chicken with salt and pepper.
4. Coat in flour; shake off any excess.
5. Dip the coated chicken into the beaten egg followed by breadcrumbs.
6. Spray the schnitzels with cooking spray.
7. Put them into the air fryer basket and cook for 10 minutes.
8. After 5 minutes, turn the schnitzels over.
9. Arrange the schnitzels on a serving platter and place the butter and lemon slices over to serve.

Honey & Mustard Glazed Drumsticks

Prep + Cook Time: 50 minutes / Servings: 4)

Nutritional info per serving:

Calories 217, Carbohydrates 10g, Fat 11g, Protein 21g

Ingredients:

1 lb drumsticks
2 tbsp honey
2 tsp dijon mustard

Salt and pepper to taste
Cooking spray

Directions:

1. Combine the honey, mustard, salt, and pepper in a large bowl.
2. Add in the chicken and toss to coat.
3. Cover and put in the fridge for 30 minutes.
4. Preheat your Cosori Air Fryer to 380 degrees F.
5. Grease the air fryer basket with cooking spray.
6. Arrange the drumsticks on the basket. Cook for 20 minutes on Air Fry mode.
7. After 10 minutes, shake the drumsticks.

Spicy Homemade Chicken Wings

(Prep + Cook Time: 25 minutes / Servings: 4)

Nutritional info per serving:

Calories 150, Carbohydrates 4g, Fat 3g, Protein 18g

Ingredients

8 chicken wings
1 tbsp ranch salad mix
1 tbsp garlic powder
1 tbsp onion powder

1 tbsp cayenne pepper
½ tsp paprika
Cooking spray

Directions:

1. Preheat your Cosori Air Fryer to 380 degrees F.
2. Combine the paprika, ranch salad mix, onion powder, garlic powder, and cayenne pepper in a bowl.
3. Pour the seasoning all over the chicken and oil with cooking spray.
4. Place in the air fryer basket and cook for 15 minutes.
5. After half of the cooking time, shake the wings. Oil the chicken again with cooking spray and continue cooking until the wings are crispy. Serve hot.

Chicken Rolls

(Prep + Cook Time: 25 minutes / Servings: 4)

Nutritional info per serving:

Calories 354, Carbohydrates 6g, Fat 18g, Protein 34g

Ingredients:

2 large chicken breasts, skinless
4 slices cheddar cheese
A handful of fresh basil leaves

4 cherry tomatoes, halved
Salt and pepper to taste
2 tbsp olive oil

Directions:

1. Preheat your Cosori Air Fryer to 370 degrees F.
2. With a sharp knife, cut a slit into the side of each chicken breast.
3. Put 2 slices of cheese, 3-4 basil leaves, and 4 cherry tomato halves into each slit.
4. Use toothpicks to keep the chicken breasts closed.
5. Season the meat with salt and pepper, and brush with some olive oil.
6. Grease the air fryer basket with the remaining olive oil and place the chicken breasts in the basket; cook for 12 minutes. After 6 minutes, turn the breasts over.
7. Once ready, leave to sit the chicken breasts, then slice each one in half and serve with salad.

Lime Chicken Kabobs

(Prep + Cook Time: 20 minutes / Servings: 4)

Nutritional info per serving:

Calories 356, Carbohydrates 53.6g, Fat 7g, Protein 20g

Ingredients:

4 chicken breasts, skinless and cubed
4 tbsp honey
Juice from 1 Lime

½ tsp ground paprika
Salt and pepper to taste

Directions:

1. Preheat your Cosori Air Fryer to 360 degrees F.

2. In a large bowl, combine the honey, soy sauce, lime juice, paprika, salt, and pepper.

3. Add in the chicken cubes and toss to coat.

4. Load 8 small skewers with honey-glazed chicken. Lay the kabobs into the air fryer basket and cook for 15 minutes. After 8 minutes, turn the kabobs over.

5. Drizzle the remaining honey sauce and serve with sautéed veggies.

Garlic & Parsley Chicken

(Prep + Cook Time: 55 minutes / Servings: 6)

Nutritional info per serving:

Calories 288, Carbohydrates 44g, Fat 18g, Protein 39g

Ingredients:

1 whole chicken, 3 lb
½ cup pitted prunes
3 minced garlic cloves
2 tbsp capers
2 bay leaves
2 tbsp red wine vinegar

2 tbsp olive oil
1 tbsp dried oregano
¼ cup packed brown sugar
1 tbsp chopped fresh parsley
Salt and black pepper to taste

Directions:

1. In a big and deep bowl, mix the prunes, olives, capers, garlic, olive oil, bay leaves, oregano, vinegar, salt, and pepper.
2. Spread the mixture on the bottom of a baking tray, and place the chicken.
3. Preheat the Cosori Air Fryer to 360° F.
4. Sprinkle a little bit of brown sugar on top of the chicken and cook for 45-55 minutes on Air Fry mode.
5. Garnish with fresh parsley.

Tasty Chicken Wings

(Prep + Cook Time: 4 hours 20 minutes / Servings: 2)

Nutritional info per serving:

Calories 287, Carbohydrates 20g, Fat 7g, Protein 26g

Ingredients:

8 chicken wings
1 tbsp water
2 tbsp potato starch

2 tbsp cornstarch
2 tbsp tom yum paste
½ tsp baking powder

Directions:

1. Combine the tom yum paste and water, in a small bowl.
2. Place the wings in a large bowl, add the tom yum mixture and coat well.
3. Cover the bowl and refrigerate for 4 hours.
4. Preheat the Cosori Air Fryer to 370 degrees F.
5. Combine the baking powder, cornstarch, and potato starch.
6. Dip each wing in the starch mixture.
7. Place on a lined baking dish in the Air fryer and cook for 7 minutes on Air Fry mode.
8. Flip over and cook for 5 to 7 minutes more.

Spiced Turkey with Cayenne Pepper

(Prep + Cook Time: 25 minutes / Servings: 6)

Nutritional info per serving:

Calories 286, Carbohydrates 6.6g, Fat 18g, Protein 24g

Ingredients:

6 turkey breasts, boneless and skinless
2 cups panko breadcrumbs
1 tsp salt
½ tsp cayenne pepper
½ tsp black pepper
1 stick butter, melted

Directions:

1. In a bowl, combine the panko breadcrumbs, half of the black pepper, the cayenne pepper, and half of the salt.
2. In another bowl, combine the melted butter with salt and pepper.
3. Brush the butter mixture over the turkey breast.
4. Coat the turkey with the panko mixture. Arrange on a lined air fryer basket.
5. Cook for 15 minutes at 390 F on Air Fry mode, flipping the meat after 8 minutes.

Chicken Cordon Bleu

(Prep + Cook Time: 40 minutes / Servings: 4)

Nutritional info per serving:

Calories 317, Carbohydrates 48g, Fat 22g, Protein 35g

Ingredients:

4 skinless and boneless chicken breasts
4 slices ham
4 slices Swiss cheese
3 tbsp all-purpose flour
4 tbsp butter
1 tsp paprika
1 tsp chicken bouillon granules
½ cup dry white wine
1 cup heavy whipping cream

Directions:

1. Preheat the Cosori Air Fryer to 380° F.
2. Pound the chicken breasts and put a slice of ham and then a slice of swiss cheese on each of the breasts. Fold the edges over the filling and secure the sides with toothpicks.
3. In a medium bowl, combine the paprika and the flour and coat the chicken pieces.
4. Fry the chicken for 20 minutes on Air Fry mode.
5. Meanwhile, in a large skillet over medium heat, melt the butter and add the bouillon and the wine. Reduce the heat to low.
6. Add in the heavy cream and let simmer for 20-25 minutes. When the chicken is done, remove to a serving platter and drizzle with the sauce. Serve hot.

Saucy Lemon Chicken

(Prep + Cook Time: 60 minutes / Servings: 2)

Nutritional info per serving:

Calories 275, Carbohydrates 19g, Fat 7.6g, Protein 36g

Ingredients:

2 chicken breasts
1 tsp minced ginger
2 rosemary sprigs
½ lemon, cut into wedges

1 tbsp soy sauce
½ tbsp olive oil
1 tbsp oyster sauce
3 tbsp brown sugar

Directions:

1. Place the ginger, soy sauce, and olive oil, in a bowl. Add the chicken and coat well.
2. Cover the bowl and refrigerate for 30 minutes.
3. Preheat the air fryer to 370 F. Transfer the marinated chicken to the air fryer basket.
4. Cook for about 6 minutes on Air Fry mode.
5. Mix the oyster sauce, rosemary and brown sugar in a small bowl. Pour the sauce over the chicken. Arrange the lemon wedges in the dish. Return to the air fryer and cook for 13 more minutes on Air Fry mode.

Mediterranean Chicken

(Prep + Cook Time: 45 minutes / Servings: 6)

Nutritional info per serving:

Calories 283, Carbohydrates 34g, Fat 12g, Protein 27g

Ingredients:

1 whole chicken (3 lb), cut in pieces
3 garlic cloves, minced
½ cup olive oil
½ cup white wine
1 tbsp fresh rosemary

1 tbsp chopped fresh oregano
1 tbsp fresh thyme
Juice from 1 lemon
Salt and black pepper, to taste

Directions:

1. Preheat the Cosori Air Fryer to 380° F.
2. In a large bowl, combine the garlic, rosemary, thyme, olive oil, lemon juice, oregano, salt, and pepper.
3. Mix all ingredients very well and spread the mixture into the air fryer basket.
4. Stir in the chicken. Sprinkle with wine and cook for 45 minutes on Air Fry mode.

Gingery Chicken Strips

(Prep + Cook Time: 35 minutes / Servings: 4)

Nutritional info per serving:

Calories 313, Carbohydrates 64g, Fat 14g, Protein 31g

Ingredients:

1 lb chicken, cut in strips
2 tomatoes, cubed
3 green peppers, cut in stripes
1 tbsp cumin powder
1 large onion

2 tbsp oil
1 tbsp mustard
1 pinch ginger
1 pinch fresh and chopped coriander
Salt and black pepper

Directions:

1. Heat the oil in a deep pan. Add in the mustard, onion, ginger, cumin and green chili peppers. Sauté the mixture for 2-3 minutes.
2. Then, add the tomatoes, coriander, and salt and keep stirring.
3. Preheat the Cosori Air Fryer to 380° F.
4. Coat the chicken with oil, salt, and pepper and cook for 25 minutes on Air Fry mode.
5. Remove from the Air Fryer and pour the sauce over and around.

Cheesy Chicken Scallopini

(Prep + Cook Time: 12 minutes / Servings: 4)

Nutritional info per serving:

Calories 218, Carbohydrates 8.9g, Fat 5.9g, Protein 30.4g

Ingredients:

4 chicken breasts, skinless and boneless
3 oz breadcrumbs
2 tbsp grated Parmesan cheese
2 oz flour
2 eggs, beaten
1 tbsp fresh, chopped sage
Cooking spray

Directions:

1. Preheat the Cosori Air Fryer to 370 degrees F.
2. Place some plastic wrap underneath and on top of the chicken breasts.
3. Using a rolling pin beat the meat until it becomes fragile.
4. In a small bowl, combine the Parmesan, sage, and breadcrumbs.
5. Dip the chicken in the egg first, and then in the sage mixture.
6. Spray with cooking oil and arrange the meat in the air fryer.
7. Cook for 7 minutes on Air Fry mode.

Chicken Tenders with Broccoli & Rice

(Prep + Cook Time: 60 minutes / Servings: 3)

Nutritional info per serving:

Calories 256, Carbohydrates 29g, Fat 15g, Protein 23g

Ingredients:

1 pound chicken tenderloins
1 package instant long grain rice
1 cup chopped broccoli

2 cups water
1 can condensed cream chicken soup
1 tbsp minced garlic

Directions:

1. Preheat the Air Fryer to 390° F, and place the chicken quarters in the Air Fryer.

2. Season with salt, pepper and a tbsp of oil and cook for 30 minutes on Roast mode.

3. Meanwhile, in a large bowl, mix rice, water, minced garlic, soup, and broccoli.

4. Combine the mixture very well.

5. Remove the chicken from the Air fryer and place it on a platter to drain.

6. Spread the rice mixture on the bottom of the dish and place the chicken on top of the rice. Cook again for 30 minutes on Roast mode.

Buttermilk Chicken Thighs

(Prep + Cook Time: 4 hours 40 minutes / Servings: 6)

Nutritional info per serving:

Calories 322, Carbohydrates 36.3g, Fat 4.2g, Protein 32.7g

Ingredients:

1 ½ lb chicken thighs
1 tsp cayenne pepper
3 tsp salt divided
2 cups flour

2 tsp black pepper
1 tbsp paprika
1 tbsp baking powder
2 cups buttermilk

Directions:

1. Rinse and pat dry the chicken thighs. Place the chicken thighs in a bowl.
2. Add cayenne pepper, 2 tsp salt, black pepper, and buttermilk, and stir to coat well.
3. Refrigerate for 4 hours. Preheat the Cosori Air Fryer to 350 degrees F.
4. In another bowl, mix the flour, paprika, 1 tsp salt, and baking powder.
5. Dredge half of the chicken thighs, one at a time, in the flour, and then place on a lined dish. Cook for 18 minutes on Air Fry mode, flipping once halfway through.
6. Repeat with the other batch.

Barbecued Chicken Satay

(Prep + Cook Time: 4h 15 minutes / Servings: 4)

Nutritional info per serving:

Calories 215, Carbohydrates 15g, Fat 8g, Protein 27g

Ingredients:

1 lb boneless,skinless chicken tenders
4 cloves garlic, chopped
4 scallions, chopped
2 tsp sesame seeds, toasted
1 tsp fresh ginger, grated

½ cup pineapple juice
½ cup soy sauce
⅓ cup sesame oil
1 pinch black pepper

Directions:

1. Skew each tender and trim any excess fat.
2. Mix the other ingredients in one large bowl.
3. Add the skewered chicken and place in the fridge for 4 to 24 hours.
4. Preheat the Cosori Air Fryer to 375 degrees F.
5. Using a paper towel, pat the chicken dry.
6. Fry for 10 minutes on Air Fry mode.

Chicken Wings with Sweet Garlic Sauce

(Prep + Cook Time: 20 minutes / Servings: 4)

Nutritional info per serving:

Calories 335, Carbohydrates 22g, Fat 24g, Protein 30g

Ingredients:

16 chicken wings
¼ cup butter
¼ cup honey

½ tsp salt
4 garlic cloves, minced
¾ cup potato starch

Directions:

1. Preheat the Cosori Air Fryer to 370 degrees F.
2. Rinse and pat dry the wings, and place in a bowl.
3. Add the starch to the bowl, and mix to coat the chicken.
4. Place the chicken in a baking dish that has been previously coated lightly with cooking oil.
5. Cook for 5 minutes on Air Fry mode.
6. Meanwhile, whisk the rest of the ingredients together in a bowl.
7. Pour the sauce over the wings and cook for another 10 minutes.

Yummy Turkey Nuggets

(Prep + Cook Time: 20 minutes / Servings: 2)

Nutritional info per serving:

Calories 423, Carbohydrates 50.9g, Fat 8.6g, Protein 34g

Ingredients:

8 oz turkey breast, boneless and skinless
1 egg, beaten
1 cup breadcrumbs

1 tbsp dried thyme
½ tsp dried parsley
Salt and pepper, to taste

Directions:

1. Preheat the Cosori Air Fryer to 350 degrees F.
2. Mince the turkey in a food processor. Transfer to a bowl.
3. Stir in the thyme and parsley, and season with salt and pepper.
4. Take a nugget-sized piece of the turkey mixture and shape it into a ball, or another form. Dip it in the breadcrumbs, then egg, then in the breadcrumbs again.
5. Place the nuggets onto a prepared baking dish. Cook for 10 minutes on Air Fry.

Cilantro Chicken Burgers

(Prep + Cook Time: 15 minutes / Servings: 8)

Nutritional info per serving:

Calories 414, Carbohydrates 27g, Fat 27g, Protein 16g

Ingredients:

1 lb ground chicken
1 red onion, chopped
1 egg, beaten
4 buns, halved
1 small red potato, shredded
A pinch of ground chili

Fresh cilantro, chopped
Salt and pepper to taste
1 Avocado, sliced
½ cup mayonnaise
1 tomato, sliced
Cooking spray

Directions:

1. Preheat your Cosori Air Fryer to 360 degrees F.
2. Mix the chicken, onion, egg, potato, chili, cilantro, salt, and pepper in a large bowl with your hands until you have an even burger mixture.
3. Shape the mixture into 8 patties. Grease your air fryer basket with cooking spray.
4. Arrange the burgers onto the basket. Cook for 10 minutes. After 5 minutes, shake the patties.
5. To assemble your burgers, spread mayonnaise on the bottom of each half of the buns, top with a chicken patty, then put over a tomato slice. Cover with the other half of the buns and arrange on a serving platter to serve.

Chicken with Greens

(Prep + Cook Time: 20 minutes / Servings: 1)

Nutritional info per serving:

Calories 551, Carbohydrates 10.7g, Fat 45g, Protein 28.7g

Ingredients:

½ cup baby spinach leaves
½ cup shredded romaine lettuce
3 large kale leaves, chopped
4 oz chicken breasts, cubed

3 tbsp olive oil, divided
1 tsp balsamic vinegar
1 garlic clove, minced
Salt and pepper, to taste

Directions:

1. Preheat the Cosori Air Fryer to 390 degrees F.
2. Place the chicken in a bowl along with 1 tbsp olive oil and garlic.
3. Season with salt and pepper; toss to combine.
4. Place on a lined baking dish and cook for 14 minutes on Roast mode in your Cosori Air Fryer.
5. Meanwhile, add the greens in a large bowl. Pour the remaining olive oil, balsamic vinegar, salt, and pepper, and toss to combine.
6. When the timer rings out, remove the chicken from the Air Fryer.
7. Arrange the greens on a serving platter and top with the chicken, to serve.

Chili Chicken Wings

(Prep + Cook Time: 25 minutes / Servings: 2)

Nutritional info per serving:

Calories 273, Carbohydrates 19g, Fat 12g, Protein 25g

Ingredients:

10 chicken wings
2 tbsp hot chili sauce
½ tbsp lime juice

½ tbsp honey
½ tsp kosher salt
½ tsp black pepper

Directions:

1. Preheat the Cosori Air Fryer to 350°F. Mix the lime juice, honey, and chili sauce.

2. Toss the mixture over the chicken wings.

3. Put the wings in the fryer's basket and cook for 25 minutes on Air Fry mode.

4. Shake the basket every 5 minutes.

BEEF, PORK & LAMB RECIPES

Apple Pork Chops

(Prep + Cook Time: 25 minutes / Servings: 3)

Nutritional info per serving:

Calories 434, Carbohydrates 30g, Fat 33g, Protein 27g

Ingredients:

Topping:

1 small onion, sliced

2 tbsp olive oil

1 tbsp apple cider vinegar

2 tsp thyme

¼ tsp brown sugar

1 cup sliced apples

2 tsp rosemary

Meat:

¼ tsp smoked paprika

1 tbsp olive oil

3 pork chops

1 tbsp apple cider vinegar

Salt and pepper, to taste

Directions:

1. Preheat the Cosori Air Fryer to 350 degrees F.
2. Place all topping ingredients in a baking dish, and then in the air fryer.
3. Cook for 4 minutes on Air Fry mode.
4. Meanwhile, place the pork chops in a bowl.
5. Add olive oil, vinegar, paprika, and season with salt and pepper.
6. Stir to coat them well. Remove the topping from the dish.
7. Add the pork chops in the dish and cook for 10 minutes on Air Fry mode.
8. Place the topping on top, return to the air fryer and cook for 5 more minutes.

Barbecued Pork Ribs

(Prep + Cook Time: 4 h 35 minutes / Servings: 2)

Nutritional info per serving:

Calories 830, Carbohydrates 22g, Fat 69g, Protein 55g

Ingredients:

1 lb pork ribs
½ tsp five spice powder
1 tsp salt
3 garlic cloves, chopped
1 tsp black pepper

1 tsp sesame oil
1 tbsp honey, plus more for brushing
4 tbsp barbecue sauce
1 tsp soy sauce

Directions:

1. Chop the ribs into smaller pieces and place in a large bowl.

2. In a separate bowl, whisk together all of the other ingredients.

3. Add to the bowl with the pork, and mix until the pork is thoroughly coated.

4. Cover the bowl, place it in the fridge, and let it marinade for about 4 hours.

5. Preheat the Cosori Air Fryer to 350 degrees F.

6. Place the ribs in the basket of the air fryer. Cook for 15 minutes on Air Fry mode.

7. After, brush the ribs with some honey and cook for 15 more minutes.

Gingery Roasted Beef

(Prep + Cook Time: 4 hours 20 minutes / Servings: 2)

Nutritional info per serving:

Calories 678, Carbohydrates 21g, Fat 39g, Protein 64g

Ingredients:

1 lb ground beef
½ tsp salt
2 tbsp soy sauce
½ tsp pepper
Thumb-sized piece of ginger, chopped
3 chilies, deseeded and chopped
4 garlic cloves, chopped

1 tsp brown sugar
Juice of 1 lime
2 tbsp mirin
2 tbsp coriander, chopped
2 tbsp basil, chopped
2 tbsp oil
2 tbsp fish sauce

Directions:

1. Place all ingredients, except beef, salt, and pepper, in a blender; pulse until smooth.
2. Season the beef with salt and pepper. Place the meat and Thai mixture in a zipper bag. Shake well to combine and let marinate in the fridge for about 4 hours.
3. Preheat the Cosori Air Fryer to 350 degrees.
4. Place the beef in the air fryer basket and cook for about 12 minutes, or more if you like it well done, on Air Fry mode. Let sit for 5 minutes before serving.

Five-Spice Roast Pork

(Prep + Cook Time: 50 minutes / Servings: 4)

Nutritional info per serving:

Calories 752, Carbohydrates 22g, Fat 69g, Protein 55g

Ingredients:

4 pork tenderloins
1 tsp five spice seasoning
½ tsp white pepper

¾ tsp garlic powder
1 tsp salt
Cooking spray

Directions:

1. Place the pork, white pepper, garlic powder, five seasoning, and salt into a bowl and toss to coat.
2. Leave to marinate at room temperature for 30 minutes.
3. Preheat the Cosori Air Fryer to 360 degrees F.
4. Place the pork into the air fryer basket, greased with cooking spray and cook for 20 minutes. After 10 minutes, turn the tenderloins.
5. Serve hot.

Herby Meatloaf

(Prep + Cook Time: 35 minutes / Servings: 8)

Nutritional info per serving:

Calories 613, Carbohydrates 18g, Fat 27g, Protein 41g

Ingredients:

4 lb ground beef
1 tbsp basil
1 tbsp oregano
1 tbsp parsley
1 onion, diced
1 tbsp Worcestershire sauce

3 tbsp ketchup
½ tsp salt
1 tsp ground peppercorns
10 whole peppercorns, for garnishing
1 cup breadcrumbs

Directions:

1. Preheat the Cosori Air Fryer to 350 degrees F. Place the beef in a large bowl.
2. Add all of the ingredients except the whole peppercorns and the breadcrumbs.
3. Mix with your hand until well combined. Stir in the breadcrumbs.
4. Put the meatloaf on a lined baking dish.
5. Insert in the air fryer and cook for 25 minutes on Air Fry mode.
6. Garnish the meatloaf with the whole peppercorns and let cool slightly before serving.

Pork Chops with Peppercorns

(Prep + Cook Time: 2 hours 20 minutes / Servings: 6)

Nutritional info per serving:

Calories 712, Carbohydrates 1.2g, Fat 82g, Protein 14g

Ingredients:

2 lb pork chops
2 bay leaves
2 tbsp soy sauce
5 garlic cloves, coarsely chopped

1 tbsp peppercorns
1 tbsp peanut oil
1 tsp salt

Directions:

1. Combine the bay leaves, soy sauce, garlic, salt, peppercorns, and oil, in a bowl.

2. Rub the mixture onto the meat. Wrap the pork with a plastic foil and refrigerate for 2 hours. Preheat the Cosori Air Fryer to 350 degrees F.

3. Place the pork in the air fryer and cook for 10 minutes on Air Fry mode. Increase the temperature to 370 F, flip the chops, and cook for another 10 minutes. Discard bay leaves before serving.

Pork Ribs with Hoisin Sauce

(Prep + Cook Time: 4 hours 55 minutes / Servings: 6)

Nutritional info per serving:

Calories 722, Carbohydrates 15g, Fat 37g, Protein 33g

Ingredients:

2 lb pork ribs
2 tbsp char siew sauce
2 tbsp minced ginger
2 tbsp hoisin sauce
2 tbsp sesame oil

1 tbsp honey
4 garlic cloves, minced
1 tbsp soy sauce

Directions:

1. Whisk together all marinade ingredients, in a small bowl.
2. Coat the ribs well with the mixture. Place in a container with a lid, and refrigerate for 4 hours. Preheat the Cosori Air Fryer to 330 degrees F.
3. Place the ribs in the basket but do not throw away the liquid from the container.
4. Cook for 40 minutes on Air Fry mode.
5. Stir in the liquid, increase the temperature to 350 F, and cook for 10 more minutes.

Rack of Lamb with Rosemary

(Prep + Cook Time: 30 minutes / Servings: 4)

Nutritional info per serving:

Calories 262 Carbohydrates 1.5g, Fat 11.8g, Protein 35g

Ingredients:

3 oz chopped cashews
1 tbsp chopped rosemary
1 ½ lb rack of lamb
1 garlic clove, minced

1 tbsp breadcrumbs
1 egg, beaten
1 tbsp olive oil
Salt and pepper, to taste

Directions:

1. Preheat the Cosori Air Fryer to 320 degrees F.
2. Combine the olive oil with the garlic and brush this mixture onto the lamb.
3. Meanwhile, combine the rosemary, cashews, and breadcrumbs, in a small bowl.
4. Brush the egg over the lambs, and then coat it with the cashew mixture.
5. Place the lamb in the air fryer and cook for 25 minutes on Air Fry mode.
6. Increase the temperature to 390 degrees F, and cook for an additional 5 minutes.
7. Cover with a foil and let sit for a couple of minutes before serving.

Appetizing Lamb Chops

(Prep + Cook Time: 30 minutes / Servings: 4)

Nutritional info per serving:

Calories 270, Carbohydrates 0.2g, Fat 13g, Protein 34.8g

Ingredients:

4 lamb chops
1 garlic clove, peeled
1 tbsp plus
2 tsp olive oil

½ tbsp oregano
½ tbsp thyme
½ tsp salt
¼ tsp black pepper

Directions:

1. Preheat the Cosori Air Fryer to 390 degrees F.
2. Coat the garlic clove with 1 tsp of olive oil and cook in the air fryer for 10 minutes on Air Fry mode.
3. Meanwhile, mix the herbs and seasonings with the remaining olive oil.
4. Using a towel, squeeze the hot roasted garlic clove into the herb mixture and stir to combine. Coat the lamb chops with the mixture well, and place in the air fryer.
5. Cook for about 8 to 12 minutes on Air Fry mode, until crispy on the outside.

Saucy Appetizer Ribs

(Prep + Cook Time: 30 minutes / Servings: 4)

Nutritional info per serving:

Calories 386, Carbohydrates 54.7g, Fat 17.5g, Protein 32.7g

Ingredients:

2 lb cut spareribs
7 oz salad dressing
5 oz canned pineapple juice
2 cups water

Garlic salt
Salt and black pepper

Directions:

1. Sprinkle the ribs with salt and pepper and place them in a saucepan.
2. Pour water and cook the ribs for around 12 minutes on high heat.
3. Drain the ribs and arrange them in the Air Fryer.
4. Sprinkle with garlic salt. Cook for 15 minutes at 390°F on Air Fry mode.
5. Meanwhile, prepare the sauce by combining the salad dressing and the pineapple juice. Serve the ribs with this delicious dressing sauce!

Spicy Beef Hamburger

(Prep + Cook Time: 40 minutes / Servings: 12)

Nutritional info per serving:

Calories 304, Carbohydrates 13g, Fat 16g, Protein 21g

Ingredients:

1 ½ lb ground beef
½ cup minced onion
2 tbsp chopped mint leaves
3 garlic cloves, minced
2 tsp paprika
2 tsp coriander seeds

½ tsp cayenne pepper
1 tsp salt
1 tbsp chopped parsley
2 tsp cumin
½ tsp ground ginger

Directions:

1. Soak 24 skewers in water, until ready to use.
2. Preheat the Cosori Air Fryer to 330 degrees F.
3. Combine all ingredients in a large bowl. Make sure to mix well with your hands until the herbs and spices are evenly distributed, and the mixture is well incorporated.
4. Shape the beef mixture into 12 shapes around 2 skewers.
5. Cook for 12 - 15 minutes on Air Fry mode, or until preferred doneness.
6. Serve with tzatziki sauce and enjoy.

Meatballs in Tomato Sauce

(Prep + Cook Time: 30 minutes / Servings: 4)

Nutritional info per serving:

Calories 255, Carbohydrates 31g, Fat 15.5g, Protein 19.5g

Ingredients:

1 cup rice
1 lb ground beef
1 onion, chopped
1 green bell pepper, finely chopped
1 tsp celery salt

2 tbsp Worcestershire sauce
1 garlic clove, minced
2 cups tomato juice
1 tsp oregano

Directions:

1. Combine the rice, ground beef, onion, celery, salt, green peppers, and garlic.

2. Shape into balls of 1 inch each.

3. Arrange the balls in the basket of the Air Fryer.

4. Cook for 15 minutes at 320°F.

5. After 8 minutes, shape the balls.

6. Heat the tomato juice, cloves, oregano, and Worcestershire sauce in a saucepan over medium heat.

7. Pour in the meatballs, bring to a boil, reduce the heat and simmer for 10 minutes, stirring often.

8. Serve warm.

Cheesy Beef & Carrot Egg Rolls

(Prep + Cook Time: 18 minutes / Servings: 3)

Nutritional info per serving:

Calories 574, Carbohydrates 51g, Fat 27.4g, Protein 28.3g

Ingredients:

1 package egg roll wrappers

1 cup ground beef

2 garlic cloves, minced

½ onion, chopped

1 large grated carrot

1 cup grated mozzarella cheese

2 tsp olive oil

¼ tsp salt

¼ tsp pepper

Directions:

1. Place the onion, garlic, carrot, and beef in a saucepan over medium heat, and cook for 6-7 minutes. Take the pan off the heat.

2. Leave to cool for a few minutes, then mix in the mozzarella. Season to taste with salt, and pepper.

3. Preheat the Cosori Air Fryer to 370 F. Grease the air fryer cooking basket with 1 tsp of the olive oil and set aside.

4. Lay the egg roll sheets onto a dry surface; divide the mixture between them.

5. Roll the egg rolls and tuck the corners and edges in to create secure rolls.

6. Lower the rolls into the air fryer cooking basket and brush them with the remaining olive oil. Cook for 13 minutes on Air Fry mode.

7. Once ready, check if the rolls are golden and crispy. Serve with green salad.

VEGETARIAN RECIPES

Minty Veggie Brochettes

(Prep + Cook Time: 20 minutes / Servings: 4)

Nutritional info per serving:

Calories 187, Carbohydrates 12g, Fat 9.4g, Protein 6.5g

Ingredients:

2 tbsp corn flour
⅔ cup canned beans
⅓ cup grated carrots
2 boiled and mashed potatoes
¼ cup chopped fresh mint leaves
½ tsp garam masala powder

½ cup paneer
1 green chili
1-inch piece of fresh ginger
3 garlic cloves
Salt, to taste

Directions:

1. Soak 12 skewers until ready to use.
2. Preheat the Cosori Air Fryer to 390 degrees F.
3. Place the beans, carrots, garlic, ginger, chili, paneer, and mint, in a food processor and process until smooth; transfer to a bowl.
4. Add the mashed potatoes, corn flour, some salt, and garam masala powder to the bowl. Mix until fully incorporated.
5. Divide the mixture into 12 equal pieces.
6. Shape each of the pieces around a skewer.
7. Cook the skewers for 10 minutes on Air Fry mode.

Potato Filled Bread Rolls

(Prep + Cook Time: 25 minutes / Servings: 4)

Nutritional info per serving:

Calories 451, Carbohydrates 93.5g, Fat 5.2g, Protein 14.2g

Ingredients:

8 slices of bread
5 large potatoes, boiled, mashed
½ tsp turmeric
2 green chilies, deseeded, chopped
1 medium onion, chopped

½ tsp mustard seeds
1 tbsp olive oil
2 sprigs curry leaf
Salt, to taste

Directions:

1. Preheat the Cosori Air Fryer to 350 degrees F. Combine the olive oil, onion, curry leaves, and mustard seed, in the air fryer basket. Cook for 5 minutes.
2. Mix the onion mixture with the mashed potatoes, chilies, turmeric, and some salt. Divide the dough into 8 equal pieces.
3. Trim the sides of the bread, and wet it with some water.
4. Make sure to get rid of the excess water. Take one wet bread slice in your palm and place one of the potato pieces in the center.
5. Roll the bread over the filling, sealing the edges.
6. Place the rolls onto a prepared baking dish, and cook for 12 minutes on Air Fry mode.

Tofu Sandwich with Red Cabbage

(Prep + Cook Time: 20 minutes / Servings: 1)

Nutritional info per serving:

Calories 225, Carbohydrates 21.5g, Fat 30.5g, Protein 12.3g

Ingredients:

2 slices of bread

1-inch thick Tofu slice

¼ cup red cabbage, shredded

2 tsp olive oil divided

¼ tsp vinegar

Salt and pepper, to taste

Directions:

1. Preheat the Cosori Air Fryer to 350 degrees F. Place the bread slices and toast for 3 minutes on Roast mode; set aside.

2. Brush the tofu with 1 tsp of oil, and place in the basket of the air fryer. Bake for 5 minutes on each side on Roast mode.

3. Combine the cabbage, remaining oil, and vinegar, and season with salt and pepper.

4. Place the tofu on top of one bread slice, place the cabbage over, and top with the other bread slice.

Chili Pepper & Sweet Potato Kebabs

(Prep + Cook Time: 20 minutes / Servings: 1)

Nutritional info per serving:

Calories 335, Carbohydrates 49.6g, Fat 14.3g, Protein 4.9g

Ingredients:

1 large sweet potato

1 beetroot

1 green bell pepper

1 tsp chili flakes

¼ tsp black pepper

½ tsp turmeric

¼ tsp garlic powder

¼ tsp paprika

1 tbsp olive oil

Directions:

1. Soak 3 to 4 skewers until ready to use.
2. Preheat the Cosori Air Fryer to 350 F.
3. Peel the veggies and cut them into bite-sized chunks.
4. Place the chunks in a bowl along with the remaining ingredients.
5. Mix until fully coated. Thread the veggies in this order: potato, pepper, beetroot.
6. Place in the air fryer and cook for 15 minutes on Air Fry mode; flip skewers halfway through.

Roasted Veggies with Penne

(Prep + Cook Time: 25 minutes / Servings: 6)

Nutritional info per serving:

Calories 391, Carbohydrates 64.4g, Fat 14.4g, Protein 9.5g

Ingredients:

1 lb penne, cooked
1 zucchini, sliced
1 pepper, sliced
1 acorn squash, sliced
4 oz mushrooms, sliced
½ cup kalamata olives, pitted, halved

¼ cup olive oil
1 tsp Italian seasoning
1 cup grape tomatoes, halved
3 tbsp balsamic vinegar
2 tbsp chopped basil
Salt and pepper, to taste

Directions:

1. Preheat the Cosori Air Fryer to 380 degrees F.
2. Combine the pepper, zucchini, squash, mushrooms, and olive oil, in a large bowl.
3. Season with salt and pepper.
4. Cook the veggies for 15 minutes on Air Fry mode.
5. In a large bowl, combine the penne, roasted vegetables, olives, tomatoes, Italian seasoning, and vinegar. Sprinkle basil and serve.

Garlic Paneer Cutlet

(Prep + Cook Time: 15 minutes / Servings: 1)

Nutritional info per serving:

Calories 567, Carbohydrates 21g, Fat 23g, Protein 19g

Ingredients:

2 cup grated paneer

1 cup grated cheese

½ tsp chai masala

1 tsp butter

½ tsp garlic powder

1 small onion, finely chopped

½ tsp oregano

½ tsp salt

Directions:

1. Preheat the Cosori Air Fryer to 350 degrees F.

2. Oil the air fryer basket.

3. Mix all ingredients in a bowl, until well incorporated.

4. Make cutlets out of the mixture and place them on the greased baking dish.

5. Place the baking dish in the air fryer and cook the cutlets for 10 minutes.

Vegetable Tortilla Pizza

(Prep + Cook Time: 15 minutes / Servings: 1)

Nutritional info per serving:

Calories 385, Carbohydrates 50.2g, Fat 12.4g, Protein 21.7g

Ingredients:

1 ½ tbsp tomato paste

¼ cup grated cheddar cheese

¼ cup grated mozzarella cheese

1 tbsp cooked sweet corn

4 zucchini slices

4 eggplant slices

4 red onion rings

½ green bell pepper, chopped

3 cherry tomatoes, quartered

1 tortilla

¼ tsp basil

¼ tsp oregano

Directions:

1. Preheat the Cosori Air Fryer to 350 degrees F. Spread the tomato paste on the tortilla.
2. Arrange the zucchini and eggplant slices first, then green peppers, and onion rings.
3. Lay the cherry tomatoes and sprinkle the sweet corn over.
4. Sprinkle with oregano and basil. Top with cheddar and mozzarella.
5. Place in the air fryer and cook for 10 minutes on Air Fry mode.

Stuffed Butternut Squash

(Prep + Cook Time: 50 minutes / Servings: 3)

Nutritional info per serving:

Calories 98, Carbohydrates 8.2g, Fat 5.3g, Protein 4.3g

Ingredients:

½ butternut squash
6 grape tomatoes, halved
1 poblano pepper, cut into strips

¼ cup grated mozzarella, optional
2 tsp olive oil divided
Salt and pepper, to taste

Directions:

1. Preheat the Cosori Air Fryer to 350 degrees F.
2. Meanwhile, cut trim the ends and cut the squash lengthwise. You will only need one half for this recipe.
3. Scoop the flash out, so you make room for the filling.
4. Brush 1 tsp oil over the squash.
5. Place in the Air fryer and roast for 30 minutes.
6. Combine the other teaspoon of olive oil with the tomatoes and poblanos.
7. Season with salt and pepper, to taste. Place the peppers and tomatoes into the squash.
8. Cook for 15 more minutes on Air Fry mode.
9. If using mozzarella, add it on top of the squash, two minutes before the end.

Peppers filled with Quinoa and Veggies

(Prep + Cook Time: 16 minutes / Servings: 1)

Nutritional info per serving:

Calories 190, Carbohydrates 29.6g, Fat 6.6g, Protein 5.7g

Ingredients:

¼ cup cooked quinoa
1 bell pepper
½ tbsp diced onion
½ diced tomato, plus one tomato slice

¼ tsp smoked paprika
Salt and pepper, to taste
1 tsp olive oil
¼ tsp dried basil

Directions:

1. Preheat the Cosori Air Fryer to 350 degrees F.
2. Core and clean the bell pepper to prepare it for stuffing. Brush the pepper with half of the olive oil on the outside.
3. In a small bowl, combine all of the other ingredients, except the tomato slice and reserved half-teaspoon olive oil.
4. Stuff the pepper with the filling. Top with the tomato slice.
5. Brush the tomato slice with the remaining half-teaspoon of olive oil and sprinkle with basil. Cook for 10 minutes on Air Fry mode.

Avocado Egg Rolls

(Prep + Cook Time: 15 minutes / Servings: 5)

Nutritional info per serving:

Calories 270, Carbohydrates 24.7g, Fat 18.7g, Protein 5.8g

Ingredients:

3 avocados, pitted and peeled
10 egg roll wrappers
1 tomato, diced

¼ tsp pepper
½ tsp salt

Directions:

1. Place all filling ingredients in a bowl. Mash with a fork until somewhat smooth.
2. Divide the feeling between the egg wrappers.
3. Wet your finger and brush along the edges so the wrappers can seal well.
4. Roll and seal the wrappers.
5. Arrange them on the lined air fryer basket, and place into the air fryer.
6. Cook at 350 degrees F, for 5 minutes on Air Fry mode.
7. Serve with chili dipping and enjoy.

Cheesy Ravioli

(Prep + Cook Time: 15 minutes / Servings: 6)

Nutritional info per serving:

Calories 298, Carbohydrates 42.1g, Fat 8.7g, Protein 13.4g

Ingredients:

1 package cheese ravioli
2 cup Italian breadcrumbs
¼ cup Parmesan cheese

1 cup buttermilk
1 tsp olive oil
¼ tsp garlic powder

Directions:

1. Preheat the Cosori Air Fryer to 390 degrees F.
2. In a bowl, combine the crumbs, Parmesan cheese, garlic powder, and olive oil.
3. Dip the ravioli in the buttermilk and then coat them with the breadcrumb mixture.
4. Line a baking sheet with parchment paper and arrange the ravioli on it.
5. Place in the air fryer and cook for 5 minutes on Air Fry mode.
6. Serve the air-fried ravioli with marinara jar sauce.

Chili Nachos

(Prep + Cook Time: 20 minutes / Servings: 2)

Nutritional info per serving:

Calories 251, Carbohydrates 25g, Fat 11.4g, Protein 8g

Ingredients:

1 cup sweet corn
1 cup all-purpose flour
1 tbsp butter

½ tsp chili powder
2-3 tbsp water
Salt to taste

Directions:

1. Add a small amount of water to the sweet corn and grind until you obtain an excellent paste. In a large bowl, add the flour, the salt, the chili powder, the butter and mix very well. Add the corn and stir well.

2. Start to knead with your palm until you obtain a stiff dough. Preheat the air fryer to 350° F. Meanwhile, dust a little bit of flour and spread the batter with a rolling pin.

3. Make it around ½ inch thick. Cut it in any shape you want and cook in the Air Fryer for 10 minutes on Air Fry mode. Serve with guacamole salsa.

Cilantro Cheese Balls

(Prep + Cook Time: 12 minutes / Servings: 2)

Nutritional info per serving:

Calories 257, Carbohydrates 31g, Fat 22g, Protein 16g

Ingredients:

2 oz paneer cheese
2 tbsp flour
2 medium onions, chopped
1 tbsp corn flour
1 green chili, chopped

A 1-inch ginger piece, chopped
1 tsp red chili powder
Cilantro leaves, chopped
Salt to taste
1 tbsp olive oil

Directions:

1. Mix all ingredients, except the oil and the cheese.
2. Take a small part of the mixture, roll it up and slowly press to flatten it.
3. Stuff in 1 cube of cheese and seal the edges. Repeat with the rest of the mixture.
4. Fry the balls in the Air Fryer for 12 minutes on Air Fry mode and at 370° F.
5. Serve hot, with ketchup.

Warm Vegetable Salad

(Prep + Cook Time: 25 minutes / Servings: 1)

Nutritional info per serving:

Calories 263, Carbohydrates 21.4g, Fat 12g, Protein 10.7g

Ingredients:

1 potato, peeled and chopped
¼ onion, sliced
1 carrot, sliced diagonally
½ small beetroot, sliced
1 cup cherry tomatoes
Juice of 1 lemon
A handful of rocket salad

A handful of baby spinach
3 tbsp canned chickpeas
½ tsp cumin
½ tsp turmeric
¼ tsp sea salt
2 tbsp olive oil
Parmesan shavings

Directions:

1. Preheat the Cosori Air Fryer to 370 degrees F.
2. Combine the onion, potato, cherry tomatoes, carrot, beetroot, cumin, seas salt, turmeric, and 1 tbsp olive oil, in a bowl.
3. Place in the air fryer and cook for 20 minutes on Air Fry mode; let cool for 2 minutes.
4. Place the rocket, salad, spinach, lemon juice, and 1 tbsp olive oil, into a serving bowl. Mix to combine; stir in the roasted veggies.
5. Top with chickpeas and Parmesan shavings.

Easy Cheese Lings

(Prep + Cook Time: 15 minutes / Servings: 4)

Nutritional info per serving:

Calories 225, Carbohydrates 23.5g, Fat 17.3g, Protein 11.6g

Ingredients:

4 cups grated cheddar cheese
1 cup all-purpose flour
1 tbsp butter
1 tbsp baking powder

¼ tsp chili powder
¼ tsp salt, to taste
1-2 tbsp water

Directions:

1. Mix the flour and the baking powder.
2. Add the chili powder, salt, butter, cheese and 1-2 tbsp of water to the mixture.
3. Make a stiff dough. Knead the dough for a while.
4. Sprinkle a tbsp or so of flour on the table.
5. Take a rolling pin and roll the dough into ½ -inch thickness.
6. Cut the dough in any shape you want.
7. Fry the cheese lings for 6 minutes at 370°F on Air Fry mode.

Crispy Kale Chips

(Prep + Cook Time: 9 minutes / Servings: 2)

Nutritional info per serving:

Calories 127, Carbohydrates 18g, Fat 10.4g, Protein 5.2g

Ingredients:

4 cups kale, stemmed and packed

2 tbsp of olive oil

1 tbsp of yeast flakes

1 tsp of vegan seasoning

Salt to taste

Directions:

1. In a bowl, add the oil, the kale, the vegan seasoning, and the yeast and mix well.

2. Dump the coated kale in the Air Fryer's basket.

3. Set the heat to 370°F and fry for a total of 6 minutes on Air Fry mode.

4. Shake it from time to time.

FISH & SEAFOOD RECIPES

Coconut & Orange Shrimp

(Prep + Cook Time: 30 minutes / Servings: 2)

Nutritional info per serving:

Calories 436, Carbohydrates 69.9g, Fat 16.4g, Protein 7.6g

Ingredients:

8 large shrimp
½ cup breadcrumbs
8 oz coconut milk
½ cup shredded coconut
¼ tsp salt
¼ tsp pepper

½ cup orange jam
1 tsp mustard
1 tbsp honey
½ tsp cayenne pepper
¼ tsp hot sauce

Directions:

1. Preheat the Cosori Air Fryer to 350 degrees F.
2. Combine the breadcrumbs, cayenne pepper, shredded coconut, salt, and pepper in a small bowl.
3. Dip the shrimp in the coconut milk, first, and then in the coconut crumbs.
4. Arrange in the lined air fryer basket, and cook for 20 minutes on Air Fry mode.
5. Meanwhile whisk the jam, honey, hot sauce, and mustard.
6. Serve the shrimp with the sauce.

Prawn & Sweet Corn Toast

(Prep + Cook Time: 12 minutes / Servings: 2)

Nutritional info per serving:

Calories 158, Carbohydrates 21g, Fat 14g, Protein 25g

Ingredients:

6 large prawns, shells removed, chopped   ½ cup sweet corn
1 large spring onion, finely sliced   1 egg white, whisked
3 white slices of bread   1 tbsp black sesame seeds

Directions:

1. In a bowl, place the prawns, corn, spring onion and the black sesame seeds.

2. Add the whisked egg white, and mix the ingredients.

3. Spread the mixture over the bread slices.

4. Place the prawns in the Air Fryer's basket and sprinkle with oil.

5. Fry the prawns until golden, for 8-10 minutes at 370° F on Air Fry mode.

6. Serve with ketchup or chili sauce.

Parsley & Paprika Tilapia

(Prep + Cook Time: 15 minutes / Servings: 4)

Nutritional info per serving:

Calories 228, Carbohydrates 1.3g, Fat 11g, Protein 32g

Ingredients:

¾ cup grated Parmesan cheese
1 tbsp olive oil
2 tsp paprika
1 tbsp chopped parsley

¼ tsp garlic powder
¼ tsp salt
4 tilapia fillets

Directions:

1. Preheat the Cosori Air Fryer to 350 degrees F.

2. Mix parsley, Parmesan, garlic, salt, and paprika, in a shallow bowl.

3. Brush the olive oil over the fillets, and then coat them with the Parmesan mixture.

4. Place the tilapia onto a lined baking sheet, and then into the air fryer.

5. Cook for about 4 to 5 minutes on all sides on Air Fry mode.

Crab Pies

(Prep + Cook Time: 55 minutes / Servings: 4)

Nutritional info per serving:

Calories 159, Carbohydrates 5.1g, Fat 10.4g, Protein 11.3g

Ingredients:

½ cup cooked crab meat
¼ cup chopped red onion
1 tbsp chopped basil
¼ cup chopped celery
¼ cup chopped red pepper
3 tbsp mayonnaise

Zest of ½ lemon
¼ cup breadcrumbs
2 tbsp chopped parsley
Old Bay seasoning, as desired
Cooking spray

Directions:

1. Preheat the Cosori Air Fryer to 390 degrees F. Place all ingredients in a large bowl and mix well until thoroughly incorporated.
2. Make 4 large crab cakes from the mixture and place on a lined sheet.
3. Refrigerate for 30 minutes, to set.
4. Spay the air basket with cooking spray and arrange the crab cakes in it.
5. Cook for 7 minutes on each side on Air Fry mode.

Dilled Salmon Fillet

(Prep + Cook Time: 13 minutes / Servings: 1)

Nutritional info per serving:

Calories 172, Carbohydrates 1.7g, Fat 7.2g, Protein 23.7g

Ingredients:

1 salmon fillet
1 tbsp fresh dill, chopped
1 tbsp soy sauce

¼ tsp garlic powder
Salt and pepper

Directions:

1. Preheat the Cosori Air Fryer to 350 degrees F.
2. Combine the soy sauce with the garlic powder, salt, dill, and pepper.
3. Brush the mixture over the salmon.
4. Place the salmon onto a sheet of parchment paper and inside the air fryer.
5. Cook for 10 minutes on Air Fry mode, until crispy on the outside and tender on the inside.

Cajun Salmon

(Prep + Cook Time: 10 minutes / Servings: 1)

Nutritional info per serving:

Calories 170, Carbohydrates 9g, Fat 7.2g, Protein 22.6g

Ingredients:

1 salmon fillet
¼ tsp brown sugar
Juice of ½ lemon

1 tbsp Cajun seasoning
2 lemon wedges
1 tbsp chopped parsley, for garnishing

Directions:

1. Preheat the Cosori Air Fryer to 350 degrees F.

2. Meanwhile, combine the sugar and lemon and coat the salmon with this mixture thoroughly.

3. Coat the salmon with the Cajun seasoning as well.

4. Place a parchment paper into the air fryer and cook the salmon for 7 minutes on Air Fry mode. If you use a thicker fillet, cook no more than 6 minutes.

5. Serve with lemon wedges and chopped parsley.

Chili Tuna Patties

(Prep + Cook Time: 50 minutes / Servings: 2)

Nutritional info per serving:

Calories 235, Carbohydrates 20.5g, Fat 6.6g, Protein 24.6g

Ingredients:

5 oz of canned tuna
1 tsp lime juice
1 tsp paprika
¼ cup flour
½ cup milk

1 small onion, diced
2 eggs
1 tsp chili powder, optional
½ tsp salt

Directions:

1. Place all ingredients in a bowl, and mix to combine.
2. Make two large patties, or a few smaller ones, out of the mixture.
3. Place them on a lined sheet and refrigerate for 30 minutes.
4. Preheat the Cosori Air Fryer to 350 degrees F.
5. Cook the patties for about 6 minutes on each side on Roast mode.

Cod Nuggets

(Prep + Cook Time: 25 minutes / Servings: 4)

Nutritional info per serving:

Calories 267, Carbohydrates 15.9g, Fat 5.8g, Protein 35.1g

Ingredients:

1 ¼ lb cod fillets, cut into chunks
½ cup flour
1 egg
1 tbsp water

1 cup cornflakes
1 tbsp olive oil
Salt and pepper, to taste

Directions:

1. Add the oil and cornflakes in a food processor, and process until crumbed.
2. Season the fish chunks with salt and pepper.
3. Beat the egg along with 1 tbsp water.
4. Dredge the chunks in flour first, then dip in the egg, and coat with cornflakes.
5. Arrange on a lined sheet. Cook at 350 degrees for 15 minutes on Air Fry mode.

Fish Sandwich with Pesto Sauce

(Prep + Cook Time: 20 minutes / Servings: 4)

Nutritional info per serving:

Calories 360, Carbohydrates 39.2g, Fat 10.4g, Protein 29.3g

Ingredients:

4 cod fillets

2 tbsp flour

10 capers

4 bread rolls

2 oz breadcrumbs

4 tbsp pesto sauce

4 lettuce leaves

Salt and pepper, to taste

Directions:

1. Preheat the Cosori Air Fryer to 370 degrees F.

2. Season the fillets with some salt and pepper, and coat them with the flour, and then dip in the breadcrumbs. You should get at the layer of breadcrumbs, that's why we don't use eggs for this recipe.

3. Arrange the fillets onto air fryer basket.

4. Cook for about 10 to 15 minutes on Air Fry mode.

5. Cut the bread rolls in half.

6. Place a lettuce leaf on top of the bottom halves; place the fillets over.

7. Spread a tbsp of pesto sauce on top of each fillet; top with the remaining halves.

Salmon Fillet with a Hazelnut Crust

(Prep + Cook Time: 15 minutes / Servings: 1)

Nutritional info per serving:

Calories 357, Carbohydrates 8.2g, Fat 23.8g, Protein 28.8g

Ingredients:

1 salmon fillet

1 tsp mustard

3 tbsp hazelnuts, chopped

A pinch of sea salt

A pinch of garlic powder

A pinch of black pepper

1 tsp lemon juice

1 tsp grated Parmesan cheese

1 tsp olive oil

Directions:

1. Preheat the Cosori Air Fryer to 350 degrees F.

2. Whisk the mustard and lemon juice together.

3. Season the salmon with salt, pepper, and garlic powder.

4. Brush the olive oil on all sides.

5. Brush the mustard-lemon mixture on top of the salmon.

6. Chop the pistachios finely, and combine them with the Parmesan cheese.

7. Sprinkle them on top of the salmon. Place the salmon in the air fryer basket with the skin side down. Cook for 10 minutes on Air Fry mode.

BREAKFAST RECIPES

Prosciutto & Mozzarella Egg Muffins

(Prep + Cook Time: 20 minutes / Servings: 2)

Nutritional info per serving:

Calories 291, Carbohydrates 12.9g, Fat 20.5g, Protein 13g

Ingredients:

2 slices bread
2 prosciutto slices, chopped
2 eggs
4 tomato slices

2 tbsp grated mozzarella
2 tbsp mayonnaise
Salt and pepper, to taste
Cooking spray

Directions:

1. Preheat the Cosori Air Fryer to 320 degrees F.

2. Grease two large ramekins with cooking spray.

3. Place one bread slice in the bottom of each ramekin.

4. Arrange 1 prosciutto slice and 2 tomato slices on top of each bread slice.

5. Divide the mozzarella between the ramekins.

6. Crack the eggs over the mozzarella.

7. Season with salt and pepper.

8. Cook for 10 minutes on Air Fry mode.

9. Top with mayonnaise.

Vanilla Berry Puffs

(Prep + Cook Time: 20 minutes / Servings: 3)

Nutritional info per serving:

Calories 255, Carbohydrates 24.5g, Fat 15.7g, Protein 4.3g

Ingredients:

3 pastry dough sheets

2 tbsp mashed strawberries

2 tbsp mashed raspberries

¼ tsp vanilla extract

2 cups cream cheese

1 tbsp honey

Directions:

1. Preheat the Cosori Air Fryer to 375 degrees F.
2. Divide the cream cheese between the dough sheets and spread it evenly.
3. In a small bowl, combine the berries, honey, and vanilla.
4. Divide the mixture between the pastry sheets.
5. Pinch the ends of the sheets, to form puff.
6. You can seal them by brushing some water onto the edges, or even better, use egg wash. Lay the puffs into a lined baking dish.
7. Place the dish into the air fryer and cook for 15 minutes on Air Fry mode.
8. Once the timer beeps, check the puffs to ensure they're puffed and golden.
9. Serve warm.

Omelet with Cheddar Cheese

(Prep + Cook Time: 10 minutes / Servings: 1)

Nutritional info per serving:

Calories 347, Carbohydrates 6g, Fat 23.2g, Protein 13.6g

Ingredients:

2 eggs

2 tbsp grated cheddar cheese

1 tsp soy sauce

½ onion, sliced

¼ tsp pepper

1 tbsp olive oil

Directions:

1. Whisk the eggs along with the pepper, onion, and soy sauce, in a bowl, until well-combined.
2. Preheat the Cosori Air Fryer to 350 F on Air Fry mode.
3. Grease a baking tray with olive oil and pour in the egg mixture. Cook for 5-6 minutes.
4. Once the timer beeps, check to ensure the eggs have set.
5. Top with the grated cheddar cheese.
6. Fold the omelet in half and serve with a green salad.

Parmesan Bagel Sandwich

(Prep + Cook Time: 6 minutes / Servings: 1)

Nutritional info per serving:

Calories 432, Carbohydrates 40.4g, Fat 25.7g, Protein 10.4g

Ingredients:

2 tbsp butter, softened

1 tsp dried basil

1 tsp dried parsley

1 tsp garlic powder

1 tbsp Parmesan cheese

Salt and pepper, to taste

1 bagel

Directions:

1. Preheat the Cosori Air Fryer to 370 F. Cut the bagel in half.
2. Place in the air fryer and cook for 3 minutes on Air Fry mode.
3. Combine the butter, Parmesan, garlic, basil, and parsley, in a small bowl.
4. Season with salt and pepper, to taste.
5. Spread the mixture onto the toasted bagel.
6. Return the bagel to the Cosori Air Fryer, and cook for an additional 3 minutes on Roast mode.
7. Serve with tangy tomato relish on the side.

Maple Pancake with Raspberry

(Prep + Cook Time: 15 minutes / Servings: 4)

Nutritional info per serving:

Calories 483, Carbohydrates 88g, Fat 4.8g, Protein 13.5g

Ingredients:

2 cups all-purpose flour
1 cup milk
3 eggs, beaten
1 tsp baking powder
1 cup brown sugar

1 ½ tsp vanilla extract
½ cup frozen raspberries, thawed
2 tbsp maple syrup
Pinch of salt
Cooking spray

Directions:

1. Preheat the Cosori Air Fryer to 390 F.
2. In a bowl, mix the sifted flour, baking powder, salt, milk, eggs, vanilla extract, sugar, and maple syrup, until smooth. Gently stir in the raspberries.
3. Grease the basket of your Air fryer with cooking spray.
4. Drop the batter into the basket.
5. Cook for 10 minutes on Air Fry mode.
6. Serve the pancake right away.

Sandwich with Ham and Cheese

(Prep + Cook Time: 10 minutes / Servings: 1)

Nutritional info per serving:

Calories 452, Carbohydrates 23g, Fat 32.3g, Protein 17g

Ingredients:

2 tsp butter

2 slices bread

2 slices American cheese

1 slice ham

Directions:

1. Preheat the Cosori Air Fryer to 370 degrees F.
2. Spread one teaspoon of butter on the outside of each of the bread slices.
3. Place one cheese slice on the inside of one bread slice, top with ham slice and another cheese slice. Cover with the second bread slice to create the sandwich.
4. Place into the air fryer basket and cook for 4 minutes on Air Fry mode.
5. Flip the sandwich and cook for an additional 4 minutes.
6. When the timer beeps, remove the sandwich, cut diagonally and serve immediately with ketchup or chutney.

Paprika Shirred Eggs

(Prep + Cook Time: 20 minutes / Servings: 2)

Nutritional info per serving:

Calories 279, Carbohydrates 1.8g, Fat 20g, Protein 20.8g

Ingredients:

2 tsp butter, for greasing

4 eggs, divided

2 tbsp heavy cream

4 slices of ham

3 tbsp Parmesan cheese

¼ tsp paprika

¼ tsp pepper

2 tsp chopped chives

Directions:

1. Preheat the Cosori Air Fryer to 320 degrees F. Grease a pie pan with the butter.
2. Arrange the ham slices on the bottom of the pan to cover it completely. Use more slices if needed.
3. Whisk one egg along with the heavy cream, salt, and pepper, in a small bowl.
4. Pour the mixture over the ham slices. Crack the other eggs over the ham.
5. Scatter Parmesan cheese over and cook for 14 minutes on Air Fry mode.
6. Sprinkle with paprika and garnish with chives.

Meaty Omelet with Mozzarella

(Prep + Cook Time: 20 minutes / Servings: 2)

Nutritional info per serving:

Calories 590, Carbohydrates 6.1g, Fat 42.5g, Protein 44g

Ingredients:

1 beef sausage, chopped
4 slices prosciutto, chopped
3 oz salami, chopped
1 cup grated mozzarella cheese

4 eggs
1 tbsp chopped onion
1 tbsp ketchup

Directions:

1. Preheat the Cosori Air Fryer to 350 degrees F on Air Fry mode.
2. Whisk the eggs with the ketchup, in a bowl. Stir in the onion.
3. Spritz the inside of the air fryer basket with a cooking spray. Add and brown the sausage for about 2 minutes.
4. Meanwhile, combine the egg mixture, mozzarella cheese, salami and prosciutto.
5. Pour the egg mixture over the sausage and stir it. Cook for about 10 minutes.
6. Once the timer beeps, ensure the omelet is just set.
7. Serve immediately.

Greek-Style Quiche

(Prep + Cook Time: 40 minutes / Servings: 2)

Nutritional info per serving:

Calories 540, Carbohydrates 10.8g, Fat 43.9g, Protein 25.8g

Ingredients:

4 eggs
½ cup chopped tomatoes
1 cup crumbled feta cheese
1 tbsp chopped basil
1 tbsp chopped oregano

¼ cup chopped kalamata olives
¼ cup chopped onion
2 tbsp olive oil
½ cup milk
Salt and pepper to taste

Directions:

1. Preheat the Cosori Air Fryer to 340 degrees F. Brush a pie pan with the olive oil.
2. Beat the eggs along with the milk, salt, and pepper.
3. Stir in all of the remaining ingredients.
4. Pour the egg mixture into the pan. Cook for 30 minutes on Air Fry mode.
5. Leave to cool before serving.

Creamed Zucchini Cups

(Prep + Cook Time: 20 minutes / Servings: 4)

Nutritional info per serving:

Calories 357, Carbohydrates 47.6g, Fat 13g, Protein 12.6g

Ingredients:

1 ½ cups flour
1 tsp cinnamon
3 eggs
2 tsp baking powder
2 tbsp sugar

1 cup milk
2 tbsp butter, melted
1 tbsp yogurt
½ cup shredded zucchini
2 tbsp cream cheese

Directions:

1. Preheat the Cosori Air Fryer to 350 F on Air Fry mode.
2. In a bowl, whisk the eggs along with the sugar, a pinch of salt, cinnamon, cream cheese, sifted flour, and baking powder.
3. In another bowl, combine all liquid ingredients. Gently mix the dry and liquid mixtures. Stir in zucchini.
4. Line the muffin tins and pour in the batter. Cook for 12 minutes.
5. Once the timer beeps, check with a toothpick to ensure the muffins are set. If necessary, return them to the Air fryer, and cook for 2-3 more minutes. Transfer to a cooling rack before serving. Serve with a scraping of butter.

Honey Bread Pudding with Hazelnuts

(Prep + Cook Time: 45 minutes / Servings: 3)

Nutritional info per serving:

Calories 529, Carbohydrates 77g, Fat 20g, Protein 13g

Ingredients:

8 slices of bread
½ cup buttermilk
¼ cup honey
1 cup milk
2 eggs
½ tsp vanilla extract

2 tbsp butter, softened
¼ cup sugar
4 tbsp raisins
2 tbsp chopped hazelnuts
Cinnamon for garnish

Directions:

1. Preheat the Cosori Air Fryer to 310 degrees F.
2. Beat the eggs along with the buttermilk, honey, milk, vanilla, sugar, and butter. Stir in raisins and hazelnuts. Cut the bread into cubes and place it in a bowl. Pour the milk mixture over the bread. Let soak for about 10 minutes.
3. Cook the bread pudding for 25 minutes on Roast mode. Leave the dessert to cool for 5 minutes, then invert onto a plate and sprinkle with cinnamon to serve.

Ham & Pineapple Pizza

(Prep + Cook Time: 15 minutes / Servings: 2)

Nutritional info per serving:

Calories 425, Carbohydrates 50.2g, Fat 15.3g, Protein 23.8g

Ingredients:

2 tortillas

8 ham slices

8 mozzarella slices

8 thin pineapple slices

2 tbsp tomato sauce

Fresh basil leaves, chopped

Directions:

1. Preheat the Cosori Air Fryer to 330 degrees F.

2. Spread each tortilla with tomato sauce.

3. Scatter over the ham, pineapple, and mozzarella.

4. Place the pizza into your air fryer basket and cook for 10 minutes on Air Fry mode.

5. When the timer beeps, remove and allow to sit for 2 minutes before slicing.

6. Sprinkle the basil over and serve with napkins.

Italian Sausage Patties

(Prep + Cook Time: 20 minutes / Servings: 4)

Nutritional info per serving:

Calories 332, Carbohydrates 6.2g, Fat 24.6g, Protein 18.6g

Ingredients:

1 lb ground Italian sausage

¼ cup breadcrumbs

1 tsp dried parsley

1 tsp red pepper Flakes

½ tsp salt

¼ tsp black pepper

¼ tsp garlic powder

1 egg, beaten

Directions:

1. Preheat the Air fryer to 350 F. Line the basket with parchment paper; set aside.

2. Combine all ingredients in a large bowl. Use your hands (clean!) to combine the mixture thoroughly. Make patties out of the sausage mixture and arrange them on the basket. Cook for 14 minutes on Air Fry mode.

3. After 7 minutes, flip each patty. Once ready, remove and serve with tzatziki sauce.

Eggplant Boats

(Prep + Cook Time: 17 minutes / Servings: 2)

Nutritional info per serving:

Calories 323, Carbohydrates 15.7g, Fat 16.4g, Protein 28.3g

Ingredients:

2 eggplants

6 ham slices, chopped

1 cup mozzarella cheese, shredded

1 tsp dried parsley

Salt and pepper, to taste

Cooking spray

Directions:

1. Preheat the Cosori Air Fryer to 330 F. Grease the air fryer basket with cooking spray; set aside.

2. Cut the eggplants lengthwise in half and scoop some of the flesh out, leaving the skin intact. Season with salt and pepper.

3. Chop the scooped flesh and mix with mozzarella cheese, salt, and pepper.

4. Divide the cheese mixture between the eggplant halves. Cover with ham slices, and sprinkle with parsley.

5. Put the eggplant in the greased basket and cook for 12 minutes on Air Fry mode.

6. Serve with a fresh salad.

DESSERT RECIPES

Chocolate Fudge Loaf

(Prep + Cook Time: 55 minutes / Servings: 8)

Nutritional info per serving:

Calories 494, Carbohydrates 65.7g, Fat 25.1g, Protein 5.6g

Ingredients:

1 cup sugar
7 oz flour, sifted
1 tbsp honey
¼ cup milk
1 tsp vanilla extract

1 oz cocoa powder
2 eggs
4 oz butter
1 orange, juice and zest

Icing:

1 oz butter, melted
4 oz powdered sugar
1 tbsp brown sugar

1 tbsp milk
2 tsp honey

Directions:

1. Preheat the Cosori Air Fryer to 350 degrees F. In a bowl, mix the dry ingredients for the fudge. Mix the wet ingredients separately. Combine the two mixtures gently.

2. Transfer the batter to a prepared air fryer basket.

3. Cook for about 35 minutes on Roast mode.

4. Once the timer beeps, check to ensure the cake is cooked.

5. For the Topping: whisk together all of the icing ingredients.

6. When the cake is cooled, coat it with the icing.

7. Let set before slicing the fudge.

Coconut and Oat Cookies

(Prep + Cook Time: 30 minutes / Servings: 4)

Nutritional info per serving:

Calories 477, Carbohydrates 73.8g, Fat 16.8g, Protein 7.4g

Ingredients:

5 ½ oz flour

1 tsp vanilla extract

3 oz sugar

½ cup oats

1 small egg, beaten

¼ cup coconut flakes

Filling:

1 oz white chocolate, melted

2 oz butter

4 oz powdered sugar

1 tsp vanilla extract

Directions:

1. Beat all cookie ingredients, with an electric mixer, except the flour.
2. When smooth, fold in the flour. Drop spoonfuls of the batter onto a prepared cookie sheet.
3. Cook in the Air fryer at 350 F for about 18 minutes on Air Fry mode; let cool.
4. Meanwhile, prepare the filling by beating all ingredients together.
5. Spread the mixture on half of the cookies.
6. Top with the other halves to make cookie sandwiches.

White Chocolate Biscuits

(Prep + Cook Time: 30 minutes / Servings: 8)

Nutritional info per serving:

Calories 167, Carbohydrates 21.3g, Fat 11.3g, Protein 0.7g

Ingredients:

6 oz self-rising flour

3 oz brown sugar

2 oz white chocolate chips

1 tbsp honey

1 ½ tbsp milk

4 oz butter

Directions:

1. Preheat the Cosori Air Fryer to 350 degrees F.

2. Beat the butter and sugar until fluffy.

3. Then, beat in the honey, milk, and flour. Gently fold in the chocolate chips.

4. Drop spoonfuls of the mixture onto a prepared cookie sheet.

5. Cook for 18 minutes on Air Fry mode.

6. Once the timer beeps, make sure the cookies are just set.

Vanilla Blueberry Cupcakes

(Prep + Cook Time: 30 minutes / Servings: 10)

Nutritional info per serving:

Calories 178, Carbohydrates 26g, Fat 7.6g, Protein 2.9g

Ingredients:

1 ½ cup flour

½ tsp salt

½ cup sugar

¼ cup vegetable oil

2 tsp vanilla extract

1 cup blueberries

1 egg

2 tsp baking powder

Yogurt, as needed

Directions:

1. Preheat the Cosori Air Fryer to 350 degrees F.

2. Combine all the flour, salt and baking powder in a bowl.

3. In a bowl, place the oil, vanilla extract, and egg. Fill the rest of the bowl with yogurt.

4. Whisk the mixture until fully incorporated. Combine the wet and dry ingredients.

5. Gently fold in the blueberries. Divide the mixture between 10 muffin cups.

6. You may need to cook in batches. Cook for 10 minutes on Air Fry mode, until nice and crispy.

Cheat Apple Crumble

(Prep + Cook Time: 30 minutes / Servings: 9)

Nutritional info per serving:

Calories 296, Carbohydrates 42.5g, Fat 13.8g, Protein 2.4g

Ingredients:

4 apples, diced
2 oz butter, melted
2 oz sugar
1 oz brown sugar

2 tsp cinnamon
1 egg, beaten
3 large puff pastry sheets
¼ tsp salt

Directions:

1. Whisk the white sugar, brown sugar, cinnamon, salt, and butter together.

2. Place the apples in a baking dish and coat them with the mixture.

3. Slide the dish into the Air fryer and cook for 10 minutes on Roast mode at 350 F.

4. Meanwhile, roll out the pastry on a floured flat surface, and cut each sheet into 6 equal pieces. Divide the apple filling between the parts.

5. Brush the edges of the pastry squares with the egg. Fold and seal the edges with a fork. Place on a lined baking sheet and cook in the fryer at 350 F for 8 minutes on Roast mode. Flip them over, increase the temperature to 390 F, and cook for 2 more minutes.

Chocolate & Pineapple Cake

(Prep + Cook Time: 50 minutes / Servings: 4)

Nutritional info per serving:

Calories 411, Carbohydrates 42g, Fat 5.1g, Protein 4g

Ingredients:

2 oz dark chocolate, grated

8 oz self-rising flour

4 oz butter

7 oz pineapple chunks

½ cup pineapple juice

1 egg

2 tbsp milk

½ cup sugar

Directions:

1. Preheat the Cosori Air Fryer to 390 degrees F. Place the butter and flour into a bowl and rub the mixture with your fingers until crumbed.

2. Stir in the pineapple, sugar, chocolate, and juice.

3. Beat the eggs and milk separately, and then add them to the batter.

4. Transfer the batter to a previously prepared (greased or lined) cake pan, and cook for 40 minutes on Roast mode.

5. Let cool for at least 10 minutes before serving.

Gluten-Free Lime Muffins

(Prep + Cook Time: 30 minutes / Servings: 6)

Nutritional info per serving:

Calories 200, Carbohydrates 14.1g, Fat 11g, Protein 11.8g

Ingredients:

2 eggs plus 1 yolk

Juice and zest of 2 limes

1 cup yogurt

¼ cup superfine sugar

8 oz cream cheese

1 tsp vanilla extract

Directions:

1. Preheat the Cosori Air Fryer to 330 degrees F.
2. With a spatula, gently combine the yogurt and cheese.
3. In another bowl, beat together the rest of the ingredients.
4. Gently fold the lime with the cheese mixture.
5. Divide the batter between 6 lined muffin tins.
6. Cook in the Air fryer for 10 minutes on Air Fry mode.

Dark Chocolate Lava Cake

(Prep + Cook Time: 20 minutes / Servings: 4)

Nutritional info per serving:

Calories 785, Carbohydrates 31.6g, Fat 60.2g, Protein 30.7g

Ingredients:

3 ½ oz butter, melted

3 ½ tbsp sugar

1 ½ tbsp self-rising flour

3 ½ oz dark chocolate, melted

2 eggs

Directions:

1. Grease 4 ramekins with butter. Preheat the Cosori Air Fryer to 375 degrees F.
2. Beat the eggs and sugar until frothy. Stir in the butter and chocolate.
3. Gently fold in the flour.
4. Divide the mixture between the ramekins and bake in the air fryer for 10 minutes on Air Fry mode.
5. Let cool for 2 minutes before turning the lava cakes upside down onto serving plates.

Ring Doughnuts

(Prep + Cook Time: 25 minutes / Servings: 4)

Nutritional info per serving:

Calories 253, Carbohydrates 42.5g, Fat 9.4g, Protein 5.6g

Ingredients:

8 oz self-rising flour

1 tsp baking powder

½ cup milk

2 ½ tbsp butter

1 egg

2 oz brown sugar

Directions:

1. Preheat the Cosori Air Fryer to 350 degrees F.

2. Beat the butter with the sugar, until smooth; beat in eggs, and milk.

3. In a bowl, combine the flour with the baking powder.

4. Gently fold the flour into the butter mixture.

5. Form donut shapes and cut off the center with cookie cutters.

6. Arrange on a lined baking sheet and cook in the Air fryer for 15 minutes on Air Fry mode.

7. Serve with whipped cream.

Air Fried Snickerdoodle Poppers

(Prep + Cook Time: 30 minutes / Servings: 6)

Nutritional info per serving:

Calories 278, Carbohydrates 75.1g, Fat 2.4g, Protein 4g

Ingredients:

1 box instant vanilla Jell-O

1 can of Pillsbury Grands Flaky Layers Biscuits

1 ½ cups cinnamon sugar

Melted butter, for brushing

Directions:

1. Preheat the Cosori Air Fryer to 350 degrees F.
2. Unroll the flaky biscuits and cut them into fourths.
3. Roll each ¼ into a ball.
4. Arrange the balls on a lined baking sheet, and cook in the Air fryer for 7 minutes, or until golden, on Air Fry mode.
5. Meanwhile, prepare the Jell-O following the package's instructions.
6. Using an injector, inject some of the vanilla pudding into each ball.
7. Brush the balls with melted butter and then coat them with cinnamon sugar.

Delicious Chocolate Soufflé

(Prep + Cook Time: 25 minutes / Servings: 2)

Nutritional info per serving:

Calories 598, Carbohydrates 50.9g, Fat 41.3g, Protein 10.3g

Ingredients:

2 eggs, whites and yolks separated
¼ cup butter, melted
2 tbsp flour

3 tbsp sugar
3 oz chocolate, melted
½ tsp vanilla extract

Directions:

1. Beat the yolks along with the sugar and vanilla extract.
2. Stir in butter, chocolate, and flour. Preheat the Cosori Air Fryer to 330 degrees F.
3. Whisk the whites until a stiff peak forms.
4. Working in batches, gently combine the egg whites with the chocolate mixture.
5. Divide the batter between two greased ramekins.
6. Cook for 14 minutes on Roast.

CONCLUSION

Still have your apron on? What are you waiting for? Throw it away along with your woks and pans, and try some of these amazingly delicious recipes the cleaner and much healthier way.

Now that you have convinced yourself that the air fryer is so much more than oil-free frying, the next step is to prepare these recipes, modify them to your liking, and create your own unique air fried delicacies.

Life awaits. Go #AirFry!

Made in the USA
San Bernardino, CA
08 November 2019